Occupy Whiteness

OCCUPY WHITENESS

Joaquín Zihuatanejo

DEEP VELLUM PUBLISHING

DALLAS, TEXAS

Deep Vellum Publishing
3000 Commerce Street, Dallas, Texas 75226
deepvellum.org · @deepvellum

Deep Vellum is a 501c3 nonprofit literary arts organization
founded in 2013 with the mission to bring
the world into conversation through literature.

Copyright ©2024 by Joaquín Zihuatanejo

Support for this publication has been provided in part by the National Endowment for the Arts, the Texas Commission on the Arts, the City of Dallas Office of Arts and Culture, the Communities Foundation of Texas, and the George and Fay Young Foundation

ISBNs: 978-1-64605-308-7 (paperback) | 978-1-64605-323-0 (ebook)

LIBRARY OF CONGRESS CATALOGING-IN-PUBLICATION DATA
Names: Zihuatanejo, Joaquín, author.
Title: Occupy whiteness.
Description: First U.S. edition. | Dallas, Texas : Deep Vellum, 2023. |
"Joaquín Zihuatanejo"--Title page verso. | Text in English and Spanish.

Identifiers: LCCN 2023042673 (print) | LCCN 2023042674 (ebook) | ISBN
9781646053087 (trade paperback) | ISBN 9781646053230 (ebook)
Subjects: LCGFT: Poetry. | Experimental poetry.
Classification: LCC PS3576.I42 O23 2023 (print) | LCC PS3576.I42 (ebook)
LC record available at https://lccn.loc.gov/2023042673
LC ebook record available at https://lccn.loc.gov/2023042674

Front Cover Design by Daniel Benneworth-Gray
Interior Layout and Typesetting by KGT

Para las que vinieron antes que nosotros
Por el rio que cruzaron
Y las cruces que llevaban

For those who came before us
For the rivers they crossed
And the crosses they bore

It responds to insult and attempted erasure simply by asserting presence
—Claudia Rankine

Que se jodan.
—Juanita

Contents

LOW KEY HIGH COUP

JUANITA SPEAKS

Author's Note

While you as the reader have the right to enter and navigate this book in any fashion that you choose, I as the poet have the right to invite you to read this collection in one of two ways.

The first is to simply read the collection from the first piece on page one until the final piece that falls on page the last.

The second is to begin with the poem "Erasure" and follow this sequence:

1. "Erasure" 2. "Este Acto de Tomar/This Act of Taking" 3. "View from the Fifth Floor of the Adam Hats Building, 1986" 4. "Air" 5. "Winter, 1984" 6. "Teresa Arrives at San Ysidro" 7. "Sestina Frontera" 8. "Eight Miles Southwest of San Miguel" 9. "You Will Make It" 10. Rooted in the Verge" 11. "Near a Dirt Road South of La Muela" 12. "She" 13. "Wake" 14. "The Row Between Us" 15. "After Drought" 16. "Incipient" 17. "Of Muskets and Maíz" 18. "Gunshots Could be Heard Inside" 19. "Guest Speaker" 20. "New STATEMENT" 21. "White Lines" 22. "Someone Heard a Cry for Help from a Trailer in the 9600 Block of Quintana Road" 23. "Fluvial Deposits" 24. "Still" 25. "The Cartels" 26. "Empty Holster" 27. "The Officers" 28. "The Crossing" 29. "South on I-45 Dallas to Huntsville" 30. "Stigma(ta)" 31. "After Reading That the Death Toll Rises to 53, I Recall a Conversation with My Abuelita Juanita About a Borracho Found Dead in the Barrio" 32. "He's Not the Only One" 33. "Home" 34. "Of Flesh and Sand"

At the request of my editor, Sebastián Páramo, I inserted micro essays, essays, and other prose pieces into the collection to embrace the hybrid form. Those pieces are unnamed and undocumented. But they exist. And they are no less important. You will note they are not on white pages. You might consider reading these as you come to them in the collection. Or simply reading the poems first and then the prose pieces.

A CONVERSATION WITH A WHITE POET
AT A PRESTIGIOUS LITERARY FESTIVAL

Them: So, let me get this straight, you take a book by a white, male author and you read it until a page jumps out at you for whatever reason. You then erase every page before it. And every page after it. Then you select somewhere between three and fourteen random words on that single page and erase all the other words. Leaving those isolated words floating in a sea of white space. You then occupy that white space with what you're calling Brown verse. Is my understanding correct?

Me: Yes. It is.

Them: But don't you feel bad about taking words, even if it's just three isolated words on a page, from a white, male author?

Me: No.

Them: Why not?

Me: Because you see I'm not taking any words. I'm discovering them. I'm colonizing them.

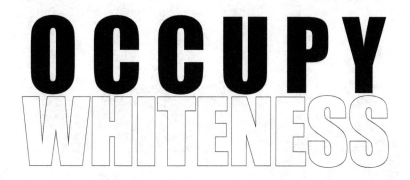

Sestina Frontera

de la misma manera / we more akin to dark than light / cursed for Spanish tongues / for whom death gapes / with bruised hands and heels / we stay low give watchmen the slip / we just another kind of silt / eso es lo que la gente quiere que le esplique / climb from river wash away silt / move quickly travel lightly / cuidado silently sideslip / wrap sharp American syllables around tongues / beware the coyote the heel / you run pant your mouth gapes / es verdad / this new country this language gap / nothing more than dreams and silt / trained dogs fresh on heels run from darkness run to light / slow your breath silence tongue / let water slip through lips / y le dirémas las mujeres   /   in dresses lower their slips / arid canyon walls gape / silence chattering teeth with tongues / use hands to carve a bed in silt / pray to the Virgin's horned moon for light / don't wish for home don't click your heels / creo que de seos solo hay uno: yo / when morning comes walk softly toe then heel / through the bosque you quietly slip /

question your prayers   do not trust   the light / la migra hungry to close the gap / smooth
out your skirt   dust off the silt / tilt heads   to ground   stifle tongues / si se deciden a
hablar / let the rolled *r*   fall   from your tongues / pick up the pace   push with your heels /
you   more than river   more than silt / more than mistake   more than slip / familia awaits

their arms agape / run   claw   fight   for the light   /   aquí está   todo suyo   /   speak
lightly   /   hold tongue   /   a gaping   /   wound called faith   here   you are healed /

baptized   by river slip   /   and   earthly silt

Not far from where I live there are students. Brown children. Born here. Living there. Children of nowhere. Their parents came over to work in the fields. These children are American citizens who live in Mexico. Their day starts with a walk to their first bus ride. Some of those students walk great distances. Hours before the sun rises. To that first bus ride. After their second bus ride they finally arrive at the border, where new policies and procedures slow them down. To a standstill. In some instances, tripling the time it used to take them to cross over. Líneas. Lines. Waiting in long lines is a part of their every day.

After crossing the border: another city bus ride to an area near the school, where they walk the last few blocks from there. Yes, some of them are sponsored by American (in most cases Mexican American) familias (families) and they live with them in Brownsville Monday through Friday and then go home on the weekends to Mexico to be with their fathers and mothers, sisters and brothers. (Which brings with it its own kind of trauma to deal with.) But there are students who make this journey every day.

Every. Day.

And if they have extracurricular activities that keep them after school: fútbol, football, ROTC, student clubs and organizations, that means their walk, their first bus ride, their crossing, their second and third bus rides, their long walk home from there . . . is delayed. Can you imagine what it is to start your day at 4 am? In the darkness of morning. To study and do homework as best you can many times while riding on multiple, crowded buses. To sacrifice in this way. To work in this way. All day. And then make the long journey home arriving sometimes at eight P.M., nine P.M., ten P.M. . . . only to wake in a handful of hours to start. All over. Again.

These are the children of the RGV. The Rio Grande Valley. A place that is both here. And there. At the same time. Perhaps I was wrong. Maybe they aren't children of nowhere. Maybe they are children of everywhere. If you ever hear a Latínx/a/o use the term *ganas*, these children . . . this story . . . is what I want you to think of.

Rooted in the Verge

for Isidro

There where grapes

and brown boys grow.

                        I opened my eyes

       vineyards

       how they grow up from ground

       and overhead.

                        I recall how impossible this

       seemed.

Hearing God

                        on still air

whisper in your ear,

You were born to be caged.

            Do you feel free

            when you taste your wine?

No need to read it in books

migrant boys can tell you

all you need to know of slavery

      rows of shack homes

      shared by multiple families

      hard dirt packed floors

      communal bathroom

      toilet stalls without doors

      because brown boys can't afford

      the privilege of privacy

      even while shitting.

                                   Clouds came full over, and

thunder

the morning storm did not linger,

                                   it drifted by languidly.

There where sons rise

but do not shine.

There where brown boys give

sweat and blood

to the soil.

They were growing

hooked onto vines

rooted in the verge.

Can you tell

where their hands end

and earth begins?

The Row Between Us

Can   poem   be

                               bandera
drenched   in   surrender?

Pull   white   pickup   off   road
and   into   the   turn   row.

                               We   come   to
dirt   in   a   close-knit   way.

Take   the   penknife   out,   jab
at   one   of   the   rows.

                               What   lies   rooted

               in   voice.

                               They
                               cotton
effortless

                               secrets   in   earth

                    ashes,   everything   sacred

lifts   up   in   flat   clod.

We

digging   a   little   deeper   uncover

                                        the   loam,

do   not   spare   the   harrow

                            wrestle   with   white,

ache   return   find
field
                            spreads

before   us.

Untiring.

                                        Fingers   bleed

                            under

                                        water   jug.

So   much   blood,

so   little   water   dry
to   replenish   this
landscape.

We   return.   Reap.

One   of   the   cotton   seeds
          sprouted   bent   double   broken.

In   October   another
grandchild born
where   only   white   grows,
only   brown

           thoughts

           we   might   not
make   it.

We   emerge   into   blinding   noon.
Son   will   not   forgive   father.

A   little   further   up   the
row   finds   the   same   thing,

32

Hello. Hello. Hell—

.

Erasure

it starts with

                            scoffs

                  the knocking over of things

hollow tree trunk ocelot skin

                        yaohuehuetl

a man speaking over a PA

          singing

          music playing

an inaudible laugh

                            gunshots firing

rubber bullets

                          water canons

a sign that reads

                    stop the removals

a lighter clicks

breath of benzene

somewhere in the distance

babies crying women screaming thunder rumbling dogs barking
whistle blowing sobbing sirens screeching footsteps approaching

and still the drums

beyond the barracades

the indistinct whispers

of white men

sound just like a restless rivulet

can something be 62 percent water and 38 percent arsenic

CUANTO HAGAS PARA LASTIMARME
NO BASTA PARA TENERTE MIEDO.

WHATEVER YOU DO TO HURT ME,
IS NOT ENOUGH TO MAKE ME FEAR YOU.

Incipient

someone   that loves

                                        the ignition of small fires

            left

to save   himself   I mean

ceiling height   and thermal layering

caused the flashover

nothing spontaneous
about this kind of combustion

I too

burned

                seven breaths until my throat seared

and yet again

we keep this   between us

and again

                 you go

                 I turn my back

                 close my eyes

                 count to ten

now fully developed

I inherit   the slag

but I will not accept   so he says

again

decay is not the most dangerous stage of fire

I softly kiss my father's cheek

whisper in his ear

I know father

but it is the longest

South on I-45 Dallas to Huntsville

Can you tell me about the prison?

Nothing

I cannot tell you
how many armed guards
are stationed in the tower,
only

blood formed from this

offense

nor can I recall
color of mortar,
maze that was
path to visitation

only your voice
los corridos
cab of Dodge
filled with song.

In the end where will I dwell?

Nothing

ends mi'jo.

We are

breath

without check.

will choose not to see you. I stand before you a Brown man who has felt the hate in their eyes. I stand before you a Brown man who has felt the barrel of a white police officer's gun against the back of my head and the only thing I was guilty of in that moment was being young, Brown, and poor. I have felt their terror first hand. All true. And you, young Black child, you will feel it too. So make stone of your flesh. Become bronze. Do everything in your power to harden yourself to prepare for their onslaught. And for the briefest of moments I thought to myself, *I'm glad I did not bring a Brown son into this world.*

Sadly, this is all true too.

My mouth opened. "Hi," I replied.

"I love police's."

"I'm sorry, what did you say?"

"I love police's. So much."

"You do?"

"Oh yes . . . so much."

"Why?" I don't know why I asked. Maybe I'm a recovering teacher who loves to learn from students who are an age that makes them so much closer to God than I am.

True.

"Oh, they are the best's, oh, they are so nice, and oh so awesome. I just love them. Wait, are you a police's?"

I caught a glimpse of myself in the mirror in front of me. This young, Black child did not see me as Brown. Did not see me as less than. My Fight Club T-shirt was of no concern to him. There was nothing suspicious in his eyes about the fact that I was in a police station washing fingerprint ink off the tips of my fingers. He saw me only as something capable of good. He saw in me the ability to be the most heroic thing in his profound brown eyes . . . a "police's."

"No," I replied. "I'm not a police officer."

"Oh . . . what are you?"

"I'm a poet." I don't normally say that. But it felt right today.

"Oh . . . that's good too. I think I will be a police's when I grow up."

"You know what, I think you will be too."

He breathed in deeply, the sound of inhalation/revelation, "You really think so?"

"I know so." I turned to leave. "Have a good day."

"You too . . . bye!"

And for the briefest of moments I ached because I did not bring a Brown son into this world.

True. True. True.

View from the Fifth Floor of the Adam Hats Building, 1986

Mi'jo   you see that

                                                   dark façade,

Magnolia Hotel
                              odd mythic creature
gentrified   pegasus,   hips
of flesh—or   semblance of flesh—   tor-
so of brick and glass,

                                                   obsidian-
clad shoulders

                                                   dominating
diminishing
                         a reflection,

                         far bigger than mannequin,
                                          opposite.
          Glass, stone, steel

                         what they call progress
we call theft.

They will come mi'jo

blue suits

      yellow dragons

            they will come and take all of this

from us.

New

STATEMENT

a backlash

                              dirt   in the   book

       the journey begins

      I can remember

                          being proud

published

                    emerged   Latínequis

The fact   this novel

  failed

              underlying   obligation

    mistakes   never   a novel(ty)

that defined the immigrant experience;

undocumented

    centerpiece   tastelessly

      insensitive

Simply put

                                    there
                    is no excuse

others   have spoken out

Guest Speaker

guilty ease

nothing more than salt and pepper silhouette

                        it all grows more and more routine

            they lock it

                                        a way

hope we forget

            he swore he could write any word he wanted

                        Sh . . .

                              the boulevard
                         would have burned him

         even his beautiful lies

could not

                    conceal

                         the ugly   truth

        he was desperate to hide

White Lines

it was

never

about feeling powerless

it

always felt

like

something too heavy

for one person to carry

alone

it would   take

at   least

two or three

shouting

to drown out

the enemy's voice

Temen nuestra brillantez.
Nunca lo olvides.

They fear our brilliance.
Never forget that.

Of Muskets and Maíz

when he

discovered her

my father   gave my mother
some of that   christopher columbus type love
conquered her   because she was beautiful
stripped her   of everything

and left her   bare

not long after this   she would curse his kiss
dig her fingers   into his flesh

not   like

he was the shore   after a long journey at sea
but for the sake of red blood   on white skin
a violent kind of forgetting   a bloodletting

this is where I come from   this is me

I am a child

of

muskets

and

maíz

OF FLESH AND SAND

Stigma(ta)

heat

speaks its own

language

between

US and them

an unforgiving   sun

distant   dying everyday

lay in the bed

of the truck

backs

pressed against

hot metal

the weight of stacked lumber

presses down

scars
on our palms

there is no word in English

or Spanish

for a miracle

that brings with it

only harm

Eight Miles Southwest of San Miguel

but boots

left uncovered by gravel

whether it be bullet

or heat of

desert

brown droplets

once red

worn leather

his forehead

his chest

his left shoulder   his right shoulder

just another kind

of crossing

Still

quiet now

                                                        no breath

                eyes   close

                everything impossibly   still

dirt under her fingernails

a throat silenced by soil

                her descanso

a saguaro cactus

in the distance

murder cannot be

casual

After Drought

the mouth of the river

runs

dry

hours past lights out

women

run

try not to   sleep

their hair

black

shined

like

can-

celled   furloughs

they carry nothing but water

                                   and their children

their mouths

       a parched ravine after drought

Teresa Arrives at San Ysidro

checking   the women's wing

                              checking   her name

she   walks down the hall

                         goes in

     the light   of her   face

                              pulled

               to gray   the auburn air

               working her

how could they not   know

she had
in her   a   child

four months after the miscarriage

still in detention still in pain   still neglected

still

¿Sabes por qué nos arrestan? ¿Por qué nos acosan? ¿Por qué nos oprimen? La respuesta es sencilla. No es porque *nosotros* seamos más grandes que *ellos*. Es porque *nosotros* somos iguales a *ellos*. El signo de igual parece un muro que se ha derrumbado. Lo único a lo que le temen más que a nosotros es el colapso de los muros que construyen.

Do you want to know why they detain us? Why they harass us? Why they oppress us? The answer is simple. Not because *us* is greater than *them*. But because *us* is equal to *them*. An equal sign looks like a wall that has fallen over. And the only thing they fear more than us, is the collapse of the walls they build.

The Officers

don't understand

we're   going to stop them

the signs
have been coming

despite the fact they want only

silence

they sip   their coffee   dumfounded by the different
effects   snow (and anything cold and white)

can have on our people

El 29 de marzo, poco antes de las 3 A.M. Un oficial de policía de raza blanca terminó con la vida de Adam Toledo con un arma de fuego.

Adam huía de la policía en al momento del disparo y portaba una pistola en la mano derecha. Abandonó la pistola detrás de una cerca de madera. Dio la vuelta con los brazos en el aire. Una señal de obediencia. Y recibió un disparo en el pecho a mano de un oficial de policía de Chicago. Murió momentos después en el lugar de los hechos.

Adam tenía trece años.

Todo esto pasó en verdad.

Yo tenía 13 años en el verano de 1984. En un campo de fútbol improvisado con cuatro conos naranjas que le robamos a la Ciudad de Dallas, una cancha que era un tercio de tierra y dos de sueños. Jugábamos contra Steve y su banda, los North Side Homies, un partido de 9-contra-9 con tacleadas. Eran más grandes que nosotros. Eran más fuertes y rápidos. Nos superaban en número y hasta se daban el lujo de intercambiar sus jugadores de vez en cuando.

Éramos nueve. Yo era el más débil y el más pequeño. Pero todos jugábamos fútbol juntos en la calle desde que éramos mocosos. Habíamos formulado jugadas complejas dibujadas sobre la tierra. En una jugada, yo era Tony Hill aventándose una *slant*. En otra, yo era Drew Pearson haciendo el *button-hook*. Jesús Santos siempre era Roger Staubach retrocediendo para lanzar una espiral tan sagrada como su nombre.

Les ganamos. Pero apenas. Lo suficiente para encabronarlos. Nos empezamos a pelear cuando Steve, el mexicano más enorme que he visto en mi vida, se le echó encima a Gustavo, nuestro líder. No recuerdo su nombre, pero el mejor amigo de Steve le entró para hacerlo un dos por uno.

Al instante, Manny volteó para gritarme, "¡Joaquín, ve por los carnales de Jorge y Gustavo!"

Corrí por tres cuadras hasta llegar a la casa de Gustavo y Jorge. Corté camino entre atajos. Crucé patios y salté rejas para hacer menos tiempo. Los hermanos mayores de Gustavo y Jorge siempre estaban saliendo y entrando del bote, así que no sabía a quién me iba a encontrar. Mientras iba llegando sin aliento a su casa, corrí por atrás y me encontré a uno de sus hermanos con Tory, un vato loco que acababa de salirse de los Marines y solo tenía tres pasiones en la vida: boxear, levantar pesas y fumar mota. Le estaban haciendo talacha a un viejo Buick Regal de 1976. Entre jadeos balbucí, "Steve y su banda . . . se madrean a . . . Gustavo . . . el llano . . . detrás de la escuela . . . Bonham."

Me dijeron que subiera al asiento de atrás. Hice lo que me dijeron. Azotaron el cofre, saltaron al coche y nos fuimos volando. No debimos tardar ni 90 minutos en llegar. De camino, Tory sacó una chata 38 special de la guantera y botó el cilindro para ver si estaba cargada.

Sí estaba.

Subieron el coche sobre la banqueta, cruzando la cancha de basquetbol, y a cierto punto fueron directo entre unos columpios viejos, hasta llegar al llano. Parecía que todo se movía en cámara lenta y simultáneamente a la velocidad del rayo, como si estuviéramos en una película de Michael Bay de bajo presupuesto, sólo que esto era la vida real.

Gustavo estaba tirado en el suelo mientras que Steve y otro tipo que era el segundo mexicano más enorme que he visto en mi vida le daban una paliza. A nuestra banda la retenían los de su banda o se peleaban con dos o más de los suyos. Manny, quien jamás le había dicho no a una pelea en su vida, estaba teniendo problemas para defenderse, pero Jesús tenía el pie sobre el cuello de un tipo, mientras le daba puñetazos a otro, a quien tenía sometido en una llave.

Salté fuera del coche. Un gordo que no vi de dónde salió me golpeó directo en la boca. Caí hacia atrás y justo cuando iba a empezar a patearme, se soltaron los balazos.

El hermano de Gustavo le había quitado la pistola a Tory y había disparado al aire cuatro veces. Todos los de su banda se dispersaron. Steve sólo se quedó congelado. Tory y el hermano de Gustavo le cayeron encima. Tory le dobló los brazos detrás de la espalda mientras el hermano de Gustavo de daba con el cacho de la pistola. Steve tenía la cara bañada en sangre. Mientras se arrastraba, Gustavo se levantó de la paliza que le habían dado y corrió a donde Steve para darle varias patadas en las costillas.

Chirriaban las sirenas. Cuando menos me di cuenta, había dos patrullas de la DPD en la esquina del parque entre la Vickery y la Henderson. Todos corrimos. El hermano de Gustavo le dio la pistola a Manny. Él y Tory saltaron de vuelta al Buick y desparecieron. Una patrulla los empezó a seguir. Los otros dos oficiales salieron y emprendieron la persecución a pie. Todos nos dividimos, pero Manny y yo corrimos juntos. Mientras corríamos, Manny me dijo, "A mí me lleva la verga si regreso a la juvenil, llévate esto." Y me dio la pistola.

Mientras dábamos vuelta hacia el callejón que corre en paralelo a Bonita Blvd, escuchamos al oficial gritando que paráramos. Esto sólo nos hizo correr con más voracidad.

Yo tenía trece años.

Escapaba de un policía blanco.

Con una pistola cargada y manchada de sangre en la mano.

Todo esto pasó en verdad.

El callejón serpenteaba a la izquierda y tire la pistola sobre un montón de basura lentamente invadido por un grupo de girasoles.

Unos meses después caminábamos cerca de esos girasoles y Manny me dijo, "Qué chistoso que las cosas crezcan mejor sobre la mugre." Tenía razón. Crecen mejor.

También nosotros.

El policía nos alcanzaba. Era un callejón sin salida. Sólo había un muro enfrente de nosotros sin manera de escalarlo a simple vista. Manny, quien corría unos diez pies enfrente de mí, debía ser mitad acróbata de parte de su madre y mitad leopardo de parte de su padre. Se pegó a la pared con el pie derecho como si nada y se impulsó a la cima del muro. Subió en un instante y desapareció.

Podía sentir al policía a mis espaldas. Después sentí el puño del policía hundiéndose atrás en mi rompevientos. Dejé que mis brazos se agitaran detrás de mí y me salí de mi jaqueta. Seguí el ejemplo de Manny, y en un instante, ya había trepado el muro también. Caí mal sobre el tobillo izquierdo. Cojeé por días, pero le dije a mi abuelo que me lastimé jugando soccer.

Siempre me dolía mentirle. Incluso si la mentira era para proteger sus sentimientos.

Yo tenía trece años.

A mí no me mataron ese día.

No merecí morir ese día.

Si aquel oficial de policía blanco me hubiera matado ese día, de haber quedado boca abajo entre la mugre, con los girasoles ondulándose hacía la luz como acostumbran, no estarían leyendo esto.

Mi pareja se hubiera enamorado de alguien más. Mis hijas se parecerían mucho más a su madre, pero para nada se parecerían a mí. Los poemas sin escribirse. Las páginas en blanco. Los estudiantes se hubieran sentado frente a otro maestro, quien pudiese o no amar el enseñar tanto como lo hago yo.

Todo esto pasó en verdad.

Adam Toledo tenía una prima mayor llamada Lupita Perez. Lupita tiene una hija de siete años que se llama Kaylah. Cada que Adam los visitaba, él trataba las muñecas de Kaylah como si fueran bebés de carne y hueso, los cargaba, les cantaba y los trataba con una ternura absoluta. Lo hacía para que Kaylah se riera. Y ella se reía. Siempre.

Adam era flaco y gracioso y amoroso.

Le encantaban las películas. Sobre todo, las de zombis.

Los chavos con los que solía juntarme:

Gustavo
Jorge
Mateo
Jesús
Jose
Red
Joe-Joe
Manny

Ninguno de ellos era un malandro. Eran chavos perdido que a veces hacían cosas malas.

Adam no era un malandro.

Adam pudiera haber sido un chavo perdido. Uno que a veces hacía cosas malas.

Pero él no estaba hecho de polvo.

Él estaba hecho de amor y deseo y carne y hueso y lágrimas y esperanzas y miedos y sueños y de lo que están hechas las estrellas y sí incluso polvo.

Él pudo haber sido maestro o mecánico o actor o esposo o padre o dentista o jubilado o mal golfista o abuelo. Él pudo haber sido su amigo algún día.

O el mío.

Él pudo haber sido todas esas cosas y más.

Pero no pudo.

Porque lo mataron.

Esa noche.

En ese callejón.

Adam tenía trece años.

Él no merecía morir esa noche.

Quisiera pensar que en los momentos antes de su muerte, él pudo entrever un girasol. Creciendo entre la mugre. Inclinándose hacia él.

Después de todo, los girasoles siempre se inclinan hacia la luz.

On the Life and Death of Adam Toledo

On March 29, shortly before three A.M., Adam Toledo was shot and killed by a white police officer.

Adam was running from the police at the time of the shooting and was carrying a gun in his right hand. He ditched the gun behind a wooden fence. Turned with his arms raised upright in the air. A submissive position. And was shot in the chest by a Chicago police officer. He died moments later on the scene.

Adam was thirteen years old.

All true.

The summer of 1984 I was thirteen years old. On a makeshift football field formed with four stolen City of Dallas orange cones and a gridiron that was one third dirt and two thirds dream, we played Steve and his crew, The North Side Homies, in a game of nine-on-nine tackle football. They were older than we were. They were faster and stronger. They outnumbered us and actually subbed in players from time to time.

There were nine of us. I was the smallest and the weakest. But we had all been playing street football together since we were mocosos. We had developed complicated plays drawn in the dirt. In one play I was Tony Hill running a slant. In another I was Drew Pearson running a button-hook. In every play Jesús Santos was Roger Staubach dropping back to throw a spiral that was as sacred as his name.

We beat them. Not by much. But enough to piss them off something fierce. The fight started when Steve, who was the biggest Mexican I had ever seen in my life, jumped Gustavo, our leader. Steve's best friend, whose name I can't remember, jumped in to make it two on one.

In an instant Manny turned and shouted to me, "Joaquín, go get Gustavo and Jorge's brothers!"

I ran the three blocks back to Gustavo and Jorge's house. I didn't run through the streets, but as the crow flies. Cutting through yards and jumping chain link fences to make good time. Gustavo and Jorge's older brothers were always in and out of the pen, so I didn't know who I would find. As I approached their house out of breath, I ran around back and there working on an old 1976 Buick Regal was one of their brothers and Tory, a vato loco who had just gotten out of the Marines and at the time had only three passions in life: lifting weights, boxing, and smoking mota. Between rapid and short breaths I muttered, "Steve and his crew . . . jumped . . . Gustavo . . . the dirt field . . . behind Bonham Elementary."

They told me to get in the backseat. I did as I was told. They slammed the hood shut and jumped in and we sped off. It must have taken us less than 90 seconds to get there. On the way, Tory pulled a snub nose .38 Special out of the glove box, flipped the cylinder open to see if it was loaded.

It was.

We drove over the curb, across the basketball blacktop, at one point driving directly through an old set of swings, onto the dirt field. Everything seemed to be simultaneously moving in slow motion and at breakneck speed like we were in some low-budget Michael Bay movie, only this was real.

Gustavo was on the ground taking a beating from Steve and some other guy who was the second biggest Mexican I had ever seen in my life. All of our crew were either being held back by multiple members of their crew or engaged in fights with two or more of them. Manny, who had never backed down from a fight in his life, was having trouble holding his own, but Jesús had his foot on one guy's neck while he punched another guy he had in a headlock into submission.

I jumped out of the car. A gordo I didn't see at all punched me directly in the mouth, I fell back, and just as he was about to kick me, the shots rang out.

Gustavo's brother had taken the gun from Tory and fired it in the air four times. Every one of their crew scattered. But Steve just froze. Tory and Gustavo's brother rushed him. Tory held his arms behind his back while Gustavo's brother pistol-whipped him. Steve's face was covered in blood. As he crawled away, Gustavo picked himself up from the beating he had taken and ran up on Steve and kicked him in the ribs for good measure.

Then the sirens rang out. Before I knew it there were two DPD squad cars at the edge of the park right where Vickery meets Henderson Ave. We all ran. Gustavo's brother handed Manny the gun. He and Tory jumped back in the Buick and were gone. One squad car trailed after them. The other two officers got out and pursued on foot. We all spread out, but Manny and I ran together. As we ran Manny said to me, "I can't fuck with Juvie again, take this." And he handed me the gun.

As we turned in to the alley that paralleled Bonita Blvd, we heard the officer shout for us to stop. This only made us run with more voracity.

I was thirteen years old.

Running from a white cop.

With a blood covered loaded gun in my hand.

All true.

The alley meandered to the left and I tossed the gun in a pile of garbage that was slowly being overtaken by a cluster of sunflowers.

Months later we would walk past those same sunflowers and Manny, would say to me, "It's funny how those things grow best in muck and filth." He was right. They did.

So did we.

The cop was gaining on us. The alley was a dead end. Just ahead of us was a brick wall that on first glance appeared to have no footing. Manny, who was running about ten feet ahead of me, had to have been one half acrobat on his mother's side and one half leopard on his father's side. He hit the wall in stride with his right foot and lunged for the top of the wall. In an instant, he was over it and gone.

I could feel the cop right behind me. Then I felt his fist crumple the back of my windbreaker. I let both of my arms flail behind me and ran right out of my jaqueta. I followed Manny's lead and in an instant

I was over the brick wall as well. I landed wrong on my left ankle. I limped for days, telling my Abuelo I had hurt it playing soccer.

It always hurt when I lied to him. Even if it was a lie to protect his feelings.

I was thirteen years old.

I was not killed that day.

I did not deserve to die that day.

Had I been killed by that white police officer that day, lying face-down in the muck and mire, sunflowers swaying toward the light as they were always wont to do, you would not be reading this.

My partner would have fallen in love with someone else. My daughters would still look more like their mother, but not at all like me. The poems unwritten. The pages blank. The students would have sat in front of another teacher who may or may not have loved teaching as much as I do.

All true.

Adam Toledo has an older cousin named Lupita Perez. Lupita has a seven year old daughter named Kaylah. Every time Adam would go to visit them, he would treat Kaylah's dolls as though they were living, breathing babies and hold them and sing to them and be absolutely gentle with them. He did this to make Kaylah laugh. Which she did. Every time.

Adam was skinny and funny and loving.

He loved movies. Especially ones with zombies in them.

The guys I used to run with:

Gustavo
Jorge
Mateo
Jesús
Jose
Red
Joe-Joe
Manny

None of them were bad boys. They were lost boys who sometimes did bad things.

Adam was not a bad boy.

Adam may have been a lost boy. Who sometimes did bad things.

But he was not formed from dust.

He was formed from love and lust and flesh and bone and tears and hopes and fears and dreams and starstuff and yes even dust.

He could have been a teacher or a soldier or a writer or a mechanic or an actor or a husband or a father or a dentist or a retiree or a bad golfer or a grandfather. He could have been your someday friend.

Or mine.

He could have been all those things and more.

But he can't.

Because he was killed.

That night.

In that alley.

Adam was thirteen years old.

He did not deserve to die that night.

I'd like to think in the moments before his death he caught a glimpse of a sunflower. Growing in the muck and mire. Leaning toward him.

After all, sunflowers always lean toward the light.

Near a Dirt Road South of La Muela

covered in

soledad

she

loose to the earth

her voice   asperous

murmurs

something

inaudible

then

gone

all that's left

an overturned metal drum
two rusty pipes
crossed with metal wire

a makeshift descanso

Someone Heard a Cry for Help from a Trailer in the 9600 Block of Quintana Road

how

                    they

        would do anyting

            to

        get across

                        so close

        dangerously so

to this place

calamitous

unfamiliar

beautiful

The Crossing

he feels it first

           in the arms   legs   lower back

sweat   dried   on   skin

        unforgiving cactus spines

    ankles   and feet

              bloody

two gallons of water
three cans of beans
a sleeve of saltine crackers

        118 degrees

     in two days   he will drink his own urine

80 miles to go

     alone

    except for the vultures   circling overhead

Wake

night falls

the river churns   groans

the woman
stands on the bottomland

enters slowly

rain comes

brings with it wind

the waves slapping
her

she feels the full weight

of the small bundle in her right hand

the large sack in her left

realizes quickly she cannot make it across the river

swims for the small island that separates

the two countries
here

and there

call the island nowhere

but the water has made both parcels so cumbersome

impossibly heavy

floats on her back to catch her breath

watches the once silent sky explode overhead

holds them both oh so tightly

the load she carries

the weight of them pulling her under

she tries so hard

everything she holds dear

clenched in her right and left hands

futile attempts

to pull them into her

wind-whipped

her once viselike grip weakens

she knows the river

             has them in its grasp

she cannot go on

call it instinct

           panicked desperation

let's her left hand open   slowly

the larger of the two sinks quickly

        into the river's muddy waters

that will be more gold than brown

when morning comes

a storm that will never pass

and still the woman shrieks

wails in agony

her mouth   throat   lungs

begin to fill with river water

she pulls the smaller of the two bags into her chest

the water   with its umber tint

takes them both

where it will

beyond the shoal

to the river island

where she will lay the small sack down

crawl back to the river's edge

the darkness

screaming

for what is gone

and what is left

she falls unconscious

she will wake

to chest compressions

the sensation of life being blown into her

mouth   throat   lungs

a violent cough

the body purges   water

turn her head to the side

in the direction of the small bundle

she will live

but not really

the waves   the poems   break

the truth   and all that lies   in the wake

it has taken me this long

because I so desperately want

the bundles to be sacks filled with photos

a cell phone   the family Bible   a pair of

shoes

and not her three-year-old son

who clings to life

and her nine-year-old daughter

lost to the water

102

and the boy

        played

    with
the mother's

            fluvial hair

        black

   her

  mosaic-frame

            burnt umber

the daughter   just

    out of

      arms reach

gone already

they found the boy in time to save him. many years
from now   someone will tell him the awful truth of
all that was lost.   the bruises on their backs.
shoulders. waists. how two women. mother. sister.
carried him. gave him their water.   on that day he
will learn   all there is to know of brown and gold

of

flesh

and

sand

Me lo han preguntado muchas veces en los últimos años:

¿Cuál es la solución? ¿Cuál es la solución al problema de la inmigración en este país?

Yo creo que me preguntan porque vivo en un estado fronterizo. Pero tal vez me lo preguntan porque soy un descendiente orgulloso de inmigrantes trabajadores del campo. Posiblemente me lo preguntan porque soy poeta. Y pese a nuestras inseguridades que a veces nos paralizan, ¿No se supone que los poetas tengamos todas las respuestas? A final de cuentas, tal vez me lo preguntan porque no queda nadie a quien preguntarle. Cualquiera que sea la razón, siempre tengo la misma respuesta:

No sé cuál sea la solución. Sólo sé cuál no es.

La solución nunca debiera significar que haya mujeres y niños muriendo en un río, en medio de un desierto debajo del implacable sol de Texas o en un tráiler haciendo hoyos con sus uñas entre el aislante y la hojalata para respirar. Hijas. Madres. Abuelas. Las familias no deberían morir en el intento de morir a esta nación de inmigrantes. Sobre todo al analizar la historia de los estados fronterizos que componen el sureste de los Estados Unidos. California, Arizona, Nuevo México, Texas. Si mi educación me ha enseñado algo, es que anexar sólo es una palabra sofisticada que significa robar.

Pero he llegado a una verdad absoluta al indagar en este tema. La solución no yace en fronteras abiertas. Tampoco yace en muros altos y alambre de púas. La solución no es negra. O blanca. La solución existe en un área gris. Casi todas las soluciones a los problemas del mundo yacen en el punto medio del debate. Nunca en los extremos. O en el otro. No está en levantar la voz. No está en guardar silencio. Sino en el diálogo respetuoso. En escuchar primero. Y hablar después.

Si poseemos algo de humanidad, llegaremos a aceptar la belleza del gris.

I have been asked many times over the last several years:

What is the answer? What is the answer to the immigration issue facing this country?

I think they ask me this because I live in a border state. But perhaps they ask me this because I'm the proud descendant of immigrant field workers. Possibly they ask me this because I'm a poet. And despite our sometimes-crippling insecurities, aren't poets supposed to have all the answers? In the end, maybe they ask me because there is no one left to ask. Whatever the reason, I always have the same answer:

I don't know what the answer is. I only know what it is not.

The answer should never mean women and children dying in a river, in the middle of a desert under an unforgiving Texas sun, or in a trailer clawing through insulation and tin with fingernails for airholes. Daughters. Mothers. Grandmothers. Families should not die trying to come into this nation of immigrants. Especially when you look closely at the history of the border states that make up the southwestern part of the United States. California, Arizona, New Mexico, Texas. If my education has taught me anything, it's that annexation is just a fancy word for theft.

But I have come to one absolute truth when exploring this issue. The answer does not lie in wide open borders. Nor does it rest in high walls and razor wire. The answer is not black. Or white. The answer lies in the gray. Almost all answers to the world's problems rest in the middle of the discussion. Not at one extreme. Or the other. Not in raised voices. Not in silence. But with respectful discourse. With listening first. And speaking second.

If there is any humanity in us at all, we will come to embrace the beauty of gray.

LOW
HIGH
KEY
COUP

Fluvial Deposits

                                                                          arms

                                                 brown

                        fluvial deposits

                                                          dismissed

                                          mothers

                        of the
                                          disappeared

Air

then silence

murder(us)

meaningless

lines in the dirt

[just another]

cycle of breath

[behind] her

She

                                                                                holds

        still

                                                crosses   herself
                                                        flesh   air

        we   feel   terror

        more deeply than grief

The Cartels

bloodshed

evokes   fear

how visceral

and appropriate

the   quiet

(that follows)

He's Not the Only One

for Martín, Age 19

languid

morning

triple digit heat

west of Juarez

he
touches the wall

Empty Holster

those men

without

speaking

come for her

she   reaches   for   her machete

Gunshots Could Be Heard Inside

for Angeli Gómez, a farm worker and a

mother

    breathes deep

   begs for a vest

            then without pausing

      enters the school

Home

a shaded garden

just off

a skyline

that conspires

to devour it

El lugar que antes llamé mi hogar queda a sólo 35 minutos de donde vivo ahora. ¿Cómo es que se siente tan lejos de mí? Distante. Hermoso. Inalcanzable. Como una estrella. Tal vez sea porque mi humilde éxito me ha llevado del cielo y el infierno de mi juventud a una ciudad universitaria 21 millas al norte de mi ciudad. Este nuevo lugar al que llamo mi hogar no sabe decidirse si es un suburbio de Dallas o su propio lugar. Pero Dallas fue/es/siempre será mi ciudad. La llamo mi ciudad porque en verdad era el único lugar que existía para un mocoso con los bolsillos llenos de sueños y una maldición dirigida al mundo atorada en la garganta. Tal vez los problemas de identidad de este lugar al que llamo hogar, encantador a más no poder con sus arroyos y árboles maduros, son lo que le dan su personalidad. Todo esto es desconcertante para mí. Y tal vez sólo es desconcertante para los que recordamos el llano donde jugábamos futbol detrás de la escuela Bonham Elementary. Les juro que esa cancha era de dos tercios de tierra y uno de sueños. Fue ahí donde me maravillaba de los tiros libres de Jesús Santos desde el medio campo. Un tiro a gol que era tan sagrado como su nombre. Lo que deben entender es que el barrio de mi juventud ya no existe. Lo gentrificaron las personas blancas nobles, decentes y *woke* que votaron por Carter, Mondale, Dukakis, Clinton, Clinton, Gore, Kerry, Obama, Obama, Clinton y Biden mientras que desplazaban a miles de personas morenas y pobres del único hogar que habían conocido para hacerle espacio a supermercados de comida orgánica que se ven tan estériles y carentes de vida como los pisos de un hospital.

Cuando pienso en el restaurante de sushi que existe donde antes estaba Jerry's Super Mercado, el terreno donde antes estaba la peluquería de Roy Hernandez hoy alberga altísimos condominios, pero en su momento fue nuestro espacio comunal para las risas, las maldiciones y los cuentos. Me entristece y me enfurece. Cada edificio que hoy existe en lo que llaman el sureste de las M Streets o el Old East Dallas fue alguna vez algo distinto. Todo lo que hoy existe en el barrio de mi juventud es más bonito que lo que alguna vez hubo ahí.

Pero nada de eso es más hermoso.

anymore. Gentrified by decent, upstanding white/woke folks who voted for Carter, Mondale, Dukakis, Clinton, Clinton, Gore, Kerry, Obama, Obama, Clinton, and Biden, all while displacing thousands of poor Brown people from the only home they had ever known to make room for organic grocery stores that look sterile and lifeless like hospital floors.

When I think about the sushi bar that rests where Jerry's Super Mercado once stood, the condominiums that high rise from the soil where Roy Hernandez' Barber Shop once offered us a communal space for laughter, cursing, and storytelling, it saddens and enrages me. Every single building that exists now in what they call southeast of the M Streets or Old East Dallas was once something else. Everything that exists now in the barrio of my youth is prettier than what was once there.

But none of it is more beautiful.

JUANITA
SPEAKS

After Reading That the Death Toll Rises to 53,
I Recall a Conversation with My Abuelita Juanita
about a Borracho Found Dead in the Barrio

her   voice

an   open

cotton boll

mi'jo it's true

every death   matters

Este Acto de Tomar / This Act of Taking

(Una Secuencia/A Sequence)

para mi Abuela/for my Grandmother

Ella

dijo que solo un hombre podía concebir una trinidad formada por un padre, un hijo y el fantasma del hijo asesinado.

She

said only a man could conceive a trinity formed of a father, a son, and the ghost of the slain son.

Ella

dijo que una de esas trinidades es imposible.

She

said one such trinity is impossible.

Ella

dijo que si miras de cerca la estatua de la Virgen Madre en el altar, verás dónde se ha astillado el vestido azul en algunos lugares. Causado sin duda por las manos de hombres irreflexivos. Revelando el yeso blanco debajo. Sólo la Virgen Madre tiene un alma sin mancha. No puede haber padre, ni hijo, ni fantasma sin una madre que les dé toda la vida.

She

said if you look at the statue of the Virgin Mother closely on the altar, you will see where the blue of her gown has chipped away in some places. Caused no doubt by the hands of thoughtless men. Revealing the white plaster beneath. Only the Virgin Mother has a soul without blemish. There can be no father, no son, no ghost without a mother to give them all life.

Ella

dijo que vendrán y nos quitarán todo esto.

She

said they will come and take all of this from us.

Ella

dijo que es una cosa tan masculina, este acto de tomar.

She

said it is such a masculine thing, this act of taking.

Ella

dijo que solo había una palabra en inglés para amor, pero hay muchas para robar.

She

said there was only one word in English for love, but there are many for theft.

Ella

dijo que está bien llorar. Simplemente no delante de ellos. Nunca delante de ellos.

She

said it's okay to cry. Just not in front of them. Never in front of them.

Ella

dijo que se jodan.

She

said fuck them.

Ella

dijo que no es pecado maldecir.

She

said it is not a sin to curse.

Ella

dijo que solo puedes odiar y amar en el idioma que se te da.

She

said you can only hate and love in the language you are given.

You Will Make It

Brown is

      madre

                a comfort

                        so deep

       it's fathomless

            relief   concern

           both

                 at the same time

Brown is

        grateful

blessed

      a chorus of women

   yet despite the harmony

  you

    clearly hear

    your
     Abuela's voice

Brown

solders us together

México y
los estados unidos

conjures   a house

a new
          life

equally eager
                                        and weary

to stay

Brown feels

el norte

before seeing it

with God-knows-what

pressed tightly to our chests

Brown

        gently moves a thick curl of black hair

   back behind her daughter's ear

                       Brown is tender

    in her body

in her

bones

Brown is

thunderous

pastoral

beautiful

a plentiful landscape

steeped in sacrifice

Brown   crosses herself

forehead

chest

left shoulder

right

journeys a thousand miles atop a freight train

for the smallest

chance at freedom

para sus hijas

Brown's voice is

        heavy

                then light

fiercely maternal

a
smile   that says

this side

or the other

in her tongue   and yours

en realidad nunca me perteneces
pero siempre te pertenecere

you never really belong to me
but I will always belong to you

Brown

lifts her head   opens her eyes

her voice

her breath

strained

whispers

tù lo harás

you will make it

Hoy. Un cuervo me cagó. Esto no es una metáfora. Es un hecho. Este poema sería más romántico y menos cierto si escribiera que fue un córvido. Pero de hecho fue un cuervo. Hay más letreros de *Black Lives Matter (las vidas negras importan)*, *El amor gana*, y *La diversidad se celebra* en las ventanas de las tiendas en Portland que ninguna otra de las ciudades principales de Estados Unidos. Llevo cuatro días aquí. No he visto ni a una sola persona de color en Portland. Hay quien podría decir que la 25ta ciudad más grande en este país no es una ciudad principal. Pero las estadísticas combinadas la sitúan como la número 18. Me encuentro una gráfica de barras en internet que refleja el porcentaje racial de la población en Portland. 74% blancos. 8% asiáticos. 6% negros. Menos de 1% indios americanos. No hay una gráfica de barra para Latinx. Latinos. Hispanos. Chicanos. Mexicanoamericanos. Mestizos. Esta otra dice Otros. Tal vez ahí es donde estemos. Es común que a un grupo de cuervos se le llame parvada, pero también se les dice bandada. Algunos de los narradores más bandidos, blancos y *woke* viven en áreas de estadísticas combinadas con 74% de blancos. Esos narradores tienen letreros en sus jardines que dicen, *Todos somos iguales, La gente y el planet están antes que el dinero, Cada mujer es dueña de su cuerpo*. Y también sus vecinos. Hay letreros por todo Portland. Ni con suerte encuentras más letreros en venta. No sé porque dicen que si te cae mierda de pájaro es de buena suerte. Yo me quedo con el consejo de mis estudiantes. *Mister, busque esa mierda en Google*. Y eso hago. Hay varias teorías. La primera búsqueda me da tres posibles respuestas: 1. Que te caguen es caótico y repugnante. Los partos son así, así que algo bueno han de tener. 2. Después de que un pájaro caga sobre ti, (Sí, el sitio en línea usa la preposición *sobre*. No usa el verbo *cagar*.) tú día no puede empeorar, así que sólo puede mejorar. 3. Todo es un asunto de probabilidades. Algo así como las probabilidades de ganarse la lotería o de que te mate un policía blanco debajo del desnivel de la North Skidmore cerca de la Interestatal no. 5. Si ves a cinco cuervos, lo que sigue es la enfermedad. Si ves a seis, lo que sigue es la muerte. Esto no es un hecho. Tal vez es una metáfora. Ciertamente, es una superstición. Pero acaso no todas las supersticiones vienen de alguna verdad. Y así como si nada—Veo

una persona de color en Portland. A cierta distancia de la esquina entre Powell &
12th. Hay un hombre negro, robusto e imponente. Es una foto en un cartel. Dice,
Prohibida la toxicidad en esta zona. Me siento dentro de Pine State Biscuits. Puedo
escuchar a los dos cocineros blancos hablándole a Alberto, quien lava trastes. No
puedo ver a Alberto desde la esquina de mi asiento. Pero puedo escucharlo. Él
está ahí. Él no es Otro. Él está ahí. Él es. Cuento que hay 29 personas blancas
comiendo biscuits y pollo frito. Mientras que me pongo de pie para salir, veo una
placa prendida a la mochila de un hombre blanco que dice, *Bienvenidos inmigran-
tes y refugiados.*

today. A crow shit on me. This is not metaphor. This is fact. This poem would
be more romantic and less true if I wrote it raven. But it was in fact a crow. There
are more BLACK LIVES MATTER, LOVE WINS, DIVERSITY IS CELEBRATED post-
ers hanging in storefront windows in Portland than any other major city in the
United States. I have been here four days. I have yet to see a person of color in
Portland. One might argue the twenty-fifth largest city in this country is not a
major city. But with a combined statistical area it comes in at eighteen. I find a
bar graph online depicting the racial makeup of Portland. 74% white. 8% Asian.
6% Black. Less than 1% American Indian. There is no bar graph labeled Latinx.
Latina. Hispanic. Chicano. Mexican American. Mestizo. There is one labeled
Other. We might be in there. A group of crows is commonly called a murder but
can also be known as a muster or a storytelling. Some of the most woke white
storytellers live in combined statistical areas that are 74% white. Those writers
too have signs in their front yards that read ALL PEOPLE ARE EQUAL, PEOPLE
& PLANET ARE VALUED OVER PROFIT, WOMEN ARE IN CHARGE OF THEIR
BODIES. As do their neighbors. There are signs everywhere in Portland. There is
no way for sign makers to keep up. I do not know why a bird shitting on you is a
sign of good fortune. I fall back on the advice of my students. *Mister, Google that
shit.* So I do. Theories vary. The first search yields me three possible answers.
1. It's messy and disgusting. So is childbirth, so there must be something good
about it. 2. After being shit upon (Yes, the website used the word *upon*. It did
not use the word *shit*.) by a bird, one's day surely cannot get worse and thus can
only get better. 3. It has everything to do with the odds. Something along the
odds of winning the lottery, or of being killed by a white police officer under the
North Skidmore Overpass near Interstate 5. If you see five crows, sickness will
follow. If you see six, death will follow. This is not fact. Perhaps it is metaphor.
Certainly, it is superstition. But aren't all superstitions rooted in truth. And just
like that—I see a person of color in Portland. Somewhere near the corner of
Powell & 12th. A striking, robust Black man. Pictured on a billboard. That reads
THIS IS A TOXIC FREE ZONE. Sitting in Pine State Biscuits I can hear the two
white cooks calling back to Alberto who is washing dishes. From the angle of

my booth, I cannot see Alberto. But I can hear him. He is there. He is not Other. He is here. He is. I count twenty-nine white people eating biscuits and fried chicken. As I stand to leave, I notice a button on a white man's backpack that reads, IMMIGRANTS AND REFUGEES ARE WELCOME.

A CONVERSATION WITH A NATIVE POET
AT A PRESTIGIOUS MFA PROGRAM

Me: I've been thinking about whether or not to cite the novels and works of nonfiction by the white, male authors I've been destroying to create these hybrid erasures. My gut says, *no*. I just want to make sure I'm doing the right thing. What do you think I should do?

Them: Joaquín, you have deconstructed the original source in a way that it has become something entirely new. This is more than erasure. It's obliteration. Followed by creation. Twelve isolated words pulled from a three-hundred-page novel does not warrant a citation.

Me: I see your point.

Them: If the roles were reversed, do you think a white, male author would acknowledge you? And there's something else to consider, inside and outside of the literary world, when have you ever felt acknowledged by a white man in your life?

Me: [Silent for several seconds . . .]

Them: Sounds like you have your answer.

Scan the QR code below to watch live performances of some of these pieces read by the author.

Acknowledgments

Grateful acknowledgment is given to the following people, retreats, and organizations for providing me with space and time to craft these poems:

The Dallas Public Library
The City of Dallas
The City of Dallas Office of Arts and Culture
Katherine and Eric Johnson
The Tasajillo Residency
Michelle Hannon
The Writer's Colony at Dairy Hollow
Annie and David Newcomer
The Newcomer Foundation
Thank you to Jake Skeets, Poem-a-Day, and Poets.org for publishing "102."
Thank you to Anhinga Press where earlier revisions of several of these poems were first published.
Thank you to Katherine Tejada for the About the Author photo and for filming the live performances of several pieces.
Thank you to Adry del Rocio, whose breathtakingly beautiful mural was captured by me in a black and white photo on page 163.
Thank you to Linda Stack-Nelson and the editing team at Deep Vellum Publishing for your patience and brilliance.
Thank you to Brian Duran-Fuentes for the work he did in translating this collection.

Thank you to the Institute of American Indian Arts where the seeds of what would become *Occupy Whiteness* would be planted and nourished. Thank you so much to Santee Frazier for your guidance and mentorship. Thank you to my MFA Cohort, especially Michaelsun

Stonesweat Knapp, for your brilliance and Light. Thank you to Natasha Carrizosa for being my sounding board for many of these poems. For being my self-appointed DPL translator. For the secondhand sunflowers. For always reaching. Much gratitude to Will Evans and the entire team at Deep Vellum Bookstore & Publishing Co. Thank you, Will, for fighting to make the Dallas Poet Laureate position a reality. Thank you for believing in me and this collection of poems/essays. And thank you for always fighting the good and just fight in our city. A wealth of gratitude to Sebastián H. Páramo, PhD, for all that you give to Deep Vellum Publishing Company and for being my editor and second set of eyes on *Occupy Whiteness*. I truly hope these poems honor my familia. To my astonishing partner, Aída, thank you. For everything. Remember all those years ago when we were teenagers, and I said to you, *you are the kind of person I could easily fall in love with . . .*

I did. I am.

And lastly, to all those who came before me. Mi familia. Mi sangre. Thank you. Thank you for being young and scared and beautiful. Thank you for that one night. Standing on the bottomland. Looking back at all that you left behind. Looking down at all that you carried with you. You didn't know it then. But you carried me with you. You carried these poems with you. You didn't have to brave the water that night. In fact, everything under the foolish moon was telling you not to cross. I imagine you approaching the river without speaking. You stop for a moment to look behind you. At all that had been. And then you look across. To El Norte. At all that was to come. Then without speaking, you entered the water. And that has made all the difference.

What You Can Do

Seek out, research, and support nonprofits and organizations that strive to help immigrants at the U.S.-Mexico border. Start with your community and expand from there. If you cannot donate time or resources, consider offering a donation to help fund a program you truly believe is doing the good and necessary work of protecting and supporting immigrant families.

NATIONAL:

Immigration Advocates

Informed Immigrant

RAICES – THE Refugee AND Immigrant Center FOR Education AND Legal Services

Miles for Migrants

ACLU

ARIZONA:

The Inn at the First Methodist Church

Catholic Community Services

Cruzando Fronteras

Kino Border Initiative

Immigration Advocates Network

Florence Immigrant & Refugee Rights Project

Arizona Coalition for Migrant Rights Resource Guide

CALIFORNIA:

Border Angels

San Diego Immigrant Rights Consortium

Center For Comparative Immigration Studies

Al Otro Lado (Border Rights Project)

Bridge of Love Across the Border

Border Support Network

Contra Viento Y Marea Comedor Tijuana

Assemblywoman Lorena Gonzalez, District 80 Refugee and Immigrant Resources

Deported Veterans Support House (DVSH)

NEW MEXICO:

National Immigration Legal Services

Sante Fe Dreamers Project

TEXAS:

National Network for Immigrant and Refugee Rights

Border Kindness

Haznos Valer - San Juan Apostol Shelter for Migrant women in Juarez

Casa Respetttrans - LGBTQ shelter (Juarez)

Annunciation House

Border Network For Human Rights

Hope Border Institute

Kino Border Institute

El Paso Immigration Collaborative, EPIC (In conjunction with Santa Fe Dreamers Project)

Las Americas Immigrant Advocacy Center

Diocesan Migrant & Refugee Services, Inc. (DMRS)

Austin Border Relief Volunteers

Sueños Sin Fronteras de Tejas

Angry Tias and Abuelas in Brownsville

Asylum Seeker Network of Support - Brownsville

Iglesia Bautista Migrant Respite Center

Lawyers For Good Government (Project Corazon)

Good Neighbor Settlement House

Iglesia Bautista West Brownsville Baptist Church

#ClosetheCamps
#Immigrad
#immigration
#bordercrossing
#WeAreSeeds

About the Author

Katherine Tejada

Joaquín Zihuatanejo is the proud descendant of immigrant field workers. In the last year, Joaquín has been awarded a $20,000 honorarium from the city of Dallas along with a $50,000 Laureate Fellowship Prize from the Academy of American Poets, all in honor of the outstanding work he has done in his city as their inaugural Dallas Poet Laureate.

The second sentence is not greater than the first. The second sentence would not be possible without the first.

Joaquín received his MFA in creative writing with a concentration in poetry from the Institute of American Indian Arts in Santa Fe, New Mexico. His work has been published in *Prairie Schooner, Yellow Medicine Review, Sonora Review, Southwestern American Literature,* and *Huizache* among other journals and anthologies. His poetry has been featured on HBO, NBC, and on NPR in *Historias* and *The National Teacher's Initiative*. Joaquín's collection *Arsonist* was awarded the 2017 Anhinga-Robert Dana Prize for Poetry as selected by Eduardo C. Corral. Joaquín has two passions in his life, his partner Aída and poetry. Always in that order.

Printed in the USA
CPSIA information can be obtained
at www.ICGtesting.com
JSHW051225090124
54981JS00002B/2